3-2-22

CAREERS WITH EARNING POTENTIAL

CAREERS WITH EARNING POTENTIAL

BECOME INVALUABLE IN THE WORKPLACE: SET YOURSELF APART

MACHINERY MAINTENANCE & REPAIR

PHARMACY TECHNICIAN

POLICE OFFICER AND DETECTIVE

WEB DEVELOPER

WELDER

THE ARTS

CAR MECHANIC

CHEF

COSMETOLOGIST

DOG GROOMER

FARMER

MASSAGE THERAPIST

PRESENTING YOURSELF

MASON CREST
PO Box 221876, Hollywood, FL 33022
(866) MCP-BOOK (toll-free) • www.masoncrest.com

Printed in the United States of America

First printing
9 8 7 6 5 4 3 2 1

Series ISBN: 978-1-4222-4479-1
Hardcover ISBN: 978-1-4222-4321-3
ebook ISBN: 978-1-4222-7485-9

Cataloging-in-Publication Data on file with the Library of Congress

Developed and Produced by National Highlights, Inc.
Production: Andy Morkes
Cover Design: Creative Tara
Layout: Priceless Digital Media

Publisher's Note: Websites listed in this book were active at the time of publication. The publisher is not responsible for websites that have changed their address or discontinued operation since the date of publication. The publisher reviews and updates the websites each time the book is reprinted.

QR CODES AND LINKS TO THIRD-PARTY CONTENT

You may gain access to certain third-party content ("Third-Party Sites") by scanning and using the QR Codes that appear in this publication (the "QR Codes"). We do not operate or control in any respect any information, products, or services on such Third-Party Sites linked to by us via the QR Codes included in this publication, and we assume no responsibility for any materials you may access using the QR Codes. Your use of the QR Codes may be subject to terms, limitations, or restrictions set forth in the applicable terms of use or otherwise established by the owners of the Third-Party Sites. Our linking to such Third-Party Sites via the QR Codes does not imply an endorsement or sponsorship of such Third-Party Sites or the information, products, or services offered on or through the Third-Party Sites, nor does it imply an endorsement or sponsorship of this publication by the owners of such Third-Party Sites.

3 8001 00156 2846

CHAPTER 1: Your First Day—and Beyond.......................... 11

CHAPTER 2: Appearance Counts 23

CHAPTER 3: Ten Traits of an Invaluable Employee 35

CHAPTER 4: How to Get Along Well with Your Boss 53

CHAPTER 5: Navigating Office Politics and Other Challenges 63

Series Glossary of Key Terms...................................... 72

Further Reading & Internet Resources............................... 75

Educational Video Links 76

Index... 77

Author Biography and Photo Credits................................ 80

KEY ICONS TO LOOK FOR:

 WORDS TO UNDERSTAND: These words with their easy-to-understand definitions will increase the reader's understanding of the text while building vocabulary skills.

 SIDEBARS: This boxed material within the main text allows readers to build knowledge, gain insights, explore possibilities, and broaden their perspectives by weaving together additional information to provide realistic and holistic perspectives.

EDUCATIONAL VIDEOS: Readers can view videos by scanning our QR codes, providing them with additional educational content to supplement the text. Examples include news coverage, moments in history, speeches, iconic sports moments, and much more!

 TEXT-DEPENDENT QUESTIONS: These questions send the reader back to the text for more careful attention to the evidence presented there.

 RESEARCH PROJECTS: Readers are pointed toward areas of further inquiry connected to each chapter. Suggestions are provided for projects that encourage deeper research and analysis.

 SERIES GLOSSARY OF KEY TERMS: This back-of-the-book glossary contains terminology used throughout this series. Words found here increase the reader's ability to read and comprehend higher-level books and articles in this field.

INTRODUCTION

You've landed a job. Congratulations! You're about to start one of the most exciting times of your life. You will get to work in a career that you trained for, learn new skills, make new friends, and earn a living. You've hit the big time.

But stop right there! Just because you've landed a job doesn't guarantee that you will be successful. You need to work very hard to develop new competencies, get along and work effectively with your coworkers, meet the expectations of your boss, and otherwise fit in. These things are important because you don't want to be just any worker on the job. You should strive to become an invaluable member of your company or organization. Try setting yourself apart from your coworkers in terms of job performance, because people who become invaluable in the workplace eventually receive more challenging and rewarding work assignments and, eventually, pay raises and promotions. After years of hard work, some new workers even become chief executive officers (CEOs) of their companies. For example, Chris Rondeau started his career as a front-desk clerk at Planet Fitness, one of the largest franchisors and operators of fitness centers in the United States. After years of hard work and promotions, he became the company's CEO in 2013. Tricia Griffith started out as an entry-level claims adjuster and eventually became the CEO of Progressive Insurance after three decades at the company.

Many people believe that it's easy to be successful at work. If that were true, everyone would be a CEO or eventually own a company. One main reason young workers have trouble on the job is that their expectations may not match those of their employer. According to surveys of employers, there are some typical unrealistic new-worker expectations:

- I can arrive a few minutes late for work every day if I get my work done.
- I can choose my work assignments.
- I can take extra time for lunch or coffee breaks if I feel like my work is on schedule.
- I have the right to not be monitored all the time by my boss.

- I get the day off on my birthday.
- I will get a pay raise and promotion within a few months of getting hired.

New hires who have one or more of these expectations will be in for a big surprise on their first day. While you should be treated respectfully and fairly, you should never expect special treatment if you're late, make your own rules regarding assignments, or think you can work in a cubicle "fort" without interacting with your boss. Unless your birthday falls on a weekend, plan to be at your job. Finally, you will need to be employed for at least a year—but often more—to receive a pay raise and promotion. Success only comes after hard work and significant time on the job.

THE NINE EXPECTATIONS OF EMPLOYERS

As you grew up, your parents had expectations for you—such as saying please and thank you, cleaning your room, and taking out the garbage. On the job, your employer will also have expectations for you. Here are nine of the most important:

- You will arrive to work on time and not leave early.
- You will be positive and enthusiastic each day.
- You will work hard regardless of the task.
- You will be honest and ethical.
- You will work well with your coworkers.
- You will respect your boss and follow their instructions.
- You will be dependable and manage your time effectively.
- You will follow all written and unwritten rules.
- You will continuously seek to improve your skills.

Starting a new job and meeting the expectations of your employer can seem daunting, but millions of people successfully enter the workforce each year. And if they did it, so can you. In this book, you'll learn everything you need to know to become invaluable in the workplace, including what to do to ace your first day and week on the job as well as how to dress and present yourself, build excellent relationships with your coworkers and boss, navigate office politics and other challenges, and much more. But the hard work is up to you. So let's get started on the road to your workplace success!

WORDS TO UNDERSTAND

body language: communicating nonverbally through unconscious or conscious movements and gestures

colleague: a coworker

flustered: stressed, confused, and anxious

human resources department: the unit of a company or other organization that is responsible for payroll, benefits, hiring, firing, addressing worker complaints, and staying up to date with tax laws

CHAPTER 1

YOUR FIRST DAY–AND BEYOND

YOUR FIRST DAY

Your first day on the job is one of the most important of your career. Everything you do or say will make an impression—good or bad. If you perform well, you have taken the first step to becoming an important and reliable member of your team. If you crash and burn on your first day—or simply fail to make any type of impression because you were shy and stayed in your cubicle all day—it's going to be hard to change your coworkers' opinions about you.

    Have you ever heard the saying "You never get a second chance to make a first impression"? It's important to keep this in mind on your first day. Janice, a paralegal at a large law firm in Los Angeles, wishes she had. "On my first day at the law firm, I was so shy," she recalls. "I barely made eye contact with anyone I was introduced to and could hardly get a sentence out." Janice describes herself as confident and outgoing, but something about being around hundreds of lawyers on that first day just made her clam up. "By the end of the first day, I realized I'd blown it," she says. "The initial signal that I sent was that I was meek, a poor communicator, and someone who couldn't be counted on to get the job done. I quickly resolved to change this perception, but it took a week or two of conversations, a can-do attitude, and good body language to start reversing the initial image I'd created. Today, I'm a senior paralegal and am assigned some of the most challenging tasks for paralegals at the firm."

TRUE OR FALSE? ARE YOU READY FOR YOUR NEW JOB?

1. You should wait a few weeks to introduce yourself to your coworkers.
2. It's ok to arrive late for work or take longer-than-approved coffee breaks if your coworkers do so.
3. You should never use your work computer for private purposes unless given permission by your company.

Test yourself as you read. See the end of this chapter for True or False Answers.

TWELVE THINGS TO DO ON YOUR FIRST DAY OF WORK

There are many things you should do on your first day on the job. Here are some tips that will help you ace day one and beyond.

Dress for success. Have you ever heard the saying "It's better to dress for the job you want rather than the one you have"? If you're unsure of what to wear on your first day of work, you should keep this adage in mind. Dressing appropriately sends a message that you take your job seriously. It can also put you in a professional mind-set from day one. You can always dress more casually if you find that the dress code is less formal. Look for more on what to wear in the office in Chapter 2.

Show up early. Arrive at your building at least fifteen minutes early so you're not flustered or late if your train is delayed, you get stuck in traffic, or another problem arises. The last thing you want to do on your first day is show up late.

When meeting your new coworkers, it's important to offer a firm handshake and a winning smile and to make good eye contact.

Meet your boss and coworkers. Check in with your boss to let them know that you've arrived. If you work at a large company, you may be asked to meet with a member of the human resources department (also referred to as HR or the HR department) to complete employment forms. At some companies, you'll receive a quick tour of the office to meet your coworkers. Smile, offer a firm (but not too firm) handshake, make good eye contact, and introduce yourself (if your boss hasn't already done so). Try to remember people's names and their job duties. Remember that your coworkers can be a big help as you navigate your new workplace.

Workers prepare packaged food at a fish market in Tokyo, Japan. The average Japanese employee works 1,719 hours per year.

COUNTRIES WHERE PEOPLE WORK THE MOST HOURS

The average employee in the United States works 1,779 hours a year, according to a study by the Organisation for Economic Co-operation and Development. That seems like a lot, but workers in Mexico toil an additional 467 hours a year (more than 10 weeks). Regardless of their country of origin, workers just out of high school or college should realize that they will spend a lot of time on the job. Gone are the days of a few classes a week, study time, and lots of opportunities for fun with friends. Here are the countries where people work the most hours each year:

1. Mexico: 2,246
2. South Korea: 2,113
3. Greece: 2,042
4. Chile: 1,988
5. Russia: 1,978
6. Turkey: 1,832
7. United States: 1,779
8. Italy: 1,725
9. Japan: 1,719
10. Canada: 1,691
11. Spain: 1,676
12. United Kingdom: 1,674
13. Australia: 1,665
14. France: 1,482
15. Germany: 1,371

Prepare an elevator pitch. Put together a thirty-second description that explains who you are, where you went to school, your current position, and whom you report to so that your coworkers can easily understand your background and how you fit in at the company. Such a pitch makes first conversations easier and allows you to connect with people who might have attended your college or share some other experience from your background.

Be enthusiastic and energetic. Don't be I-just-won-the-lottery enthusiastic and energetic, but speak clearly, with energy, and at a good volume. Make appropriate eye contact and stand or sit up straight. These actions send a message that you're excited about the job and working at the company. Things to avoid: crossing your arms (which makes you look unhappy or not open to new things), slouching, not making eye contact, and giving one-word answers to questions.

Learn the layout of your office. Identify the locations of the copy room, break room, elevator, etc., so that you can do your work efficiently. Determine where you can go and not go. The last thing you want to do is accidentally walk into the CEO's office during a big meeting.

Be yourself. Don't try to impress your coworkers or boss by being cocky, bragging about your work at past jobs or internships, or acting differently than you normally would. You want people to like you for who you are rather than some imagined persona.

Get to work. You'll impress your boss if you begin working right after you receive your first assignment. If you complete the task and your boss is in a meeting or on the phone, read the employee or department manual, become more familiar with the layout of the office, or meet some more coworkers. On your first day (and even during your first week), it's a good idea to keep your breaks shorter than the allotted time, and stay fifteen or so minutes late to show that you are committed to the job.

Listen and observe. While you should be friendly and get to know your colleagues and boss, you should also spend a lot of time listening to others.

Keep any strong opinions to yourself, soak up the culture of the company, and learn how everything works.

Put your cell phone on silent mode and do not use the internet for nonbusiness purposes. The last thing you want to do is appear distracted. Your boss and other coworkers deserve 100 percent of your attention.

Check in with your boss frequently during your first day to make sure you are meeting their expectations.

Stay in touch with your boss. This sounds obvious, but on your first day, you may be called to fill out forms in the HR department or get into a long conversation with the office manager or other new colleagues. You don't want your supervisor to look for you and find you missing. To avoid this issue, check in with your boss during the day. Let them know if you've been called to the HR department or must complete another task that will take you away from your desk. Check in before you head to lunch to make sure they don't need you to complete a task before you leave.

Be positive at the end of the day. Don't be too hard on yourself if you made a mistake (e.g., called someone by the wrong name, had trouble learning new software, walked into someone's cubicle by mistake, etc.). It takes time to understand the ropes. Learn from your mistakes so that your second day is much better than your first.

SOFT SKILLS: A KEY TO JOB SUCCESS

Technical knowledge and industry-specific skills are important for job success, but you also need soft skills. The National Association of Colleges and Employers recently asked hiring managers what soft skills they seek evidence of on candidates' résumés. You can be assured that any trait an employer wants to see on a résumé is also important for new workers. Here are the most crucial:

- Written communication skills (cited by 82.0% of respondents)
- Problem-solving skills (80.9%)
- The ability to work in a team (78.7%)
- Initiative (74.2%)
- Analytical/quantitative abilities (71.9%)
- A strong work ethic (70.8%)
- Verbal communication skills (67.4%)
- Leadership skills (67.4%)
- A detail-oriented personality (59.6%)

YOUR FIRST WEEK ON THE JOB

Now that you've successfully completed your first day, it's time to tackle the rest of the workweek. Here are a few things you should do during this time:

- Continue to introduce yourself to any coworkers you missed greeting.
- As you build your knowledge and take on new tasks, ask your boss and colleagues questions about work processes, your company's goals and customers, new software, and any other topics that will help you become a better worker.
- Learn how your manager likes to communicate (e.g., via email, phone, unannounced visits to their office, etc.), and see if it's ok to ask questions one at a time or if they prefer that you ask them all at once.

Work hard to develop good relationships with your coworkers.
They can be of great help as you learn the ropes at your new job.

- Build personal relationships. Ask a colleague you've connected with out for coffee or lunch. Building good relationships helps you understand the workplace culture and be more productive.

- Is your commute going smoothly? If not, leave home earlier and/or try out different modes of transportation (e.g., bus, car, train, walking). Having plenty of time and knowing multiple ways to get to work will give you peace of mind when your daily commute hits a roadblock (e.g., bad weather, traffic jam, late train, etc.).

- Add value. Do something as simple as refilling the paper in the copy machine without being asked or something more involved such as preparing a proposal to make a workplace task more efficient. The sooner you become known as a problem solver, the faster you'll move up within the organization.

- At the end of the week, prepare a status update for your supervisor that summarizes your accomplishments, lists questions that you could not find answers to on your own, and states your goals for the next week. This shows that you are detail-oriented, organized, enthusiastic, and proactive.

Learn what to do during your first ninety days on the job.

YOUR FIRST MONTH ON THE JOB—AND BEYOND

At the one-month point, you've begun to settle into your job. Hopefully, you've gotten to know your coworkers and boss and started to become an important member of your team. But your work isn't over yet. Here are a few things to do during this time:

- Continue to build relationships with your colleagues—especially members of your team.
- Learn about company departments that have no direct connection to yours; this will help you better understand how your organization works.
- Check in with your boss for a mini-assessment of how you're doing on the job. Work to identify any areas that need improvement.
- Increase your contributions at team meetings and in other settings where organizational strategies and goals are discussed. The first few weeks of a new job are for listening and learning, but at the one-month point, you should start contributing ideas.

By the one-month mark, you should feel comfortable presenting your ideas in meetings.

- Take advantage of any continuing education classes that your company offers to develop new skills and build your professional network.
- Find a mentor. Some organizations pair each new hire with a more experienced worker who teaches them the ropes and provides advice on work issues. But if your organization does not, try to identify one of the stars of your company—someone who is confident, well respected, and known as a high achiever. Try to get to know them and build a relationship, but don't force a bond that isn't there.

TRUE OR FALSE ANSWERS: ARE YOU READY FOR YOUR NEW JOB?

1. You should wait a few weeks to introduce yourself to your coworkers. **False.** You want to begin building relationships as soon as possible. Additionally, waiting a few weeks to introduce yourself sends a message that you're aloof (snobby) or lack confidence.

2. It's ok to arrive late for work or take longer-than-approved coffee breaks if your coworkers do so.
False. Never copy the actions of others if they're breaking the rules. It's especially important as a new hire to develop a reputation as someone who can be counted on and who does not flout the company policy.

3. You should never use your work computer for private purposes unless given permission by your company.
True. You can even lose your job if you misuse the internet on company time. In fact, 26 percent of companies surveyed by the American Management Association have fired workers for inappropriately using the internet.

RESEARCH PROJECT

What are five of your fears (e.g., no one liking you, being late for work, etc.) about your first day on the job? What can you do to deal with these issues before you start? Write a 300-word report that assesses each fear and presents strategies to address them.

TEXT-DEPENDENT QUESTIONS

1. Why is it important to make a good first impression at work?

2. Why is it important to build personal relationships with your colleagues?

3. Why should you send a status update to your boss at the end of your first week on the job?

befuddled: utterly confused

casual Friday: a day established by many employers in which employees are allowed to wear more casual clothing rather than business suits and dresses; also known as **dress-down Friday**

cognitive tests: those that assess the intellectual capability of people

pocket square: a small decorative piece of silk, lightweight cotton, or linen that is folded and placed in the breast pocket of a suit jacket

CHAPTER 2

APPEARANCE COUNTS

AMARI'S WARDROBE LESSON

Amari thought he had it all figured out. He had just been hired as a financial analyst at a bank. It was his first job out of college. "I'm really excited," he told his friend Marcus as they met for a cup of coffee. "A new job, good pay, and I can get my own apartment." On his first day, Amari walked into the office with a big smile on his face. He just couldn't help it. But his smile was returned with stares as he walked to his cubicle. Amari received the same reaction from his boss: a long stare, then a look of disbelief. Amari wondered what was wrong. However, as he interacted with more people during the day, he realized that he was the only one wearing khakis and a polo shirt. Everyone else was dressed in a business suit.

"How could you have made such a mistake?" his friend Marcus asked later as they had dinner.

"I dressed well for the interview, but I read online that the company had a casual dress code," Amari responded.

"They were probably talking about **casual Fridays**," Marcus said. "Or maybe they didn't know what they were talking about. You can't believe everything you read on the internet."

It was only one day, but the damage was done. Amari had failed to get the correct intel on what was appropriate in his office, and by dressing too casually, he sent the message that he wasn't ready for the big time. It took many weeks of wearing his best suits and working extra hard to change people's initial perception of him.

TRUE OR FALSE? ARE YOU AN APPEARANCE EXPERT?

1. It's a good idea to periodically check your work clothing for excessive wear or other issues.
2. Casual Friday rules are the same regardless of where you work.
3. Having a tattoo is fine in all workplaces.

Test yourself as you read. See the end of this chapter for True or False Answers.

DRESS FOR SUCCESS

Amari is not alone. Many new hires fail to understand their organization's dress code. Dressing inappropriately can cause your coworkers and boss to lose respect for you and even affect your chances of advancement. Eighty percent of executives surveyed by the staffing firm OfficeTeam said that an employee's style of dress influenced their chances of promotion. Eight percent of executives said that job attire "significantly" affected an employee's likelihood of advancement. Seventy-two percent said it "somewhat" affected their prospects.

How you dress could also affect your job performance. Just consider the findings from the following surveys and studies:

- Seventy-seven percent of managers surveyed by workwear provider Simon Jersey said that they would be less likely to offer a job to someone who was inappropriately dressed. Seventy-three percent cited a connection between how a person dresses and their attitude on the job.

- Research published in *Social Psychological and Personality Science* found that study subjects who wore formal clothing performed better on **cognitive tests** than those who wore casual clothes. According to *Scientific American*, "wearing formal business attire increased abstract thinking—an important aspect of creativity and long-term strategizing. The experiments suggest the effect is related to feelings of power."

- Research published in the *Journal of Experimental Social Psychology* found that people who wore a white lab coat made half as many mistakes on an attention-demanding task than those who did not.

WARDROBE DO'S AND DON'TS

Dressing well at work might seem overwhelming, but it's really not. If you follow these rules, you'll make a strong impression:

- Wear clean, pressed clothing.
- Never wear clothing that is too tight, too short, or too revealing.
- Wear clothing that is complementary to your body type.
- Periodically check your work wardrobe to make sure each item is free of stains, rips, or excessive wear.
- Consider introducing a dash of personality to your suit by adding an attractive **pocket square**.
- Shine your shoes.

- Know how to tie and wear a tie. The end of the tie should fall just at the top of your belt. Consult fashion websites and magazines for current width and style trends. Never tuck a tie into your slacks.
- Wear colors that match.
- Don't overdo it with jewelry, especially pieces that make a lot of noise when you move.
- Think twice before wearing short-sleeved dress shirts in the summer; many people consider them unprofessional.
- Wear denim only if it is acceptable in your workplace, and follow these denim rules: dark, straight leg, and never ripped. If you wear denim, consider offsetting this look with a blazer in a contrasting color.
- Avoid wearing statement pieces such as loud ties, Hawaiian shirts, or running shoes paired with a business suit.
- Purchase clothing with a classic look that will never go out of style.
- Spend the extra money to buy clothing that is made from quality fabrics; these clothes will last longer (if cared for properly) than less-expensive garments—saving you money in the long term.

Wearing a t-shirt with a sports jacket is not an appropriate wardrobe choice for a business setting.

Selecting work clothing that has a classic look means you won't have to purchase new outfits when styles change.

- If you can't find store-bought clothes that fit you correctly (if you're very tall, short, or overweight), consider hiring a tailor to custom-make your garments.

PERSONAL GROOMING

The importance of personal grooming is sometimes taken for granted. Everyone takes a shower, right? Wrong. During your time in the workforce, you will encounter people who do not bathe regularly or otherwise do not maintain their personal appearance. This is a mistake because poor grooming habits—whether you like it or not—suggest to others that you do not respect yourself, are inattentive to details, and don't care how you appear to others. When you are well groomed, you send a message that you are on top of your game, are professional, and get things done. Here are some basic rules to follow to present yourself professionally in the office:

This man's beard is well groomed, but his hair is too messy for a corporate setting.

- Be sure to bathe each day.
- Take good care of your nails, including getting a manicure on a regular basis. If you plan to wear open-toed shoes, get a pedicure.
- Make sure that your hair is professionally cut in a modern style.
- Men should neatly trim any facial hair.
- Do not wear excessive amounts of perfume or cologne.

Casual Friday rules may allow polo shirts and other casual clothing (pictured here) or involve much more formal wardrobe requirements.

- Visit a dentist twice a year to have your teeth cleaned. Some people keep an extra toothbrush and tube of toothpaste at the office so that they can keep their teeth clean and guard against bad breath during the workday.

CASUAL FRIDAY

On casual Friday, you can wear clothing (such as khaki pants and polo shirts) that is more relaxed than the typical business suit. Companies and other organizations have established this practice to reward employees for working hard and dressing well during the rest of the week. Casual Friday rules vary greatly by employer, so it's important to check with your boss before donning a t-shirt, shorts, and gym shoes (a bad idea!). Some companies provide information on their casual Friday policies in their employee handbooks.

Surveys show that workers continue to be **befuddled** by casual Friday policies. Forty-one percent of office workers surveyed by OfficeTeam said they were sometimes uncertain whether their clothing choices were appropriate for the office. Another finding from the survey was surprising: 48 percent of workers said that they would prefer to eliminate the uncertainty of choosing casual dress by being required to wear a uniform. "When it comes to dress codes, it's important that employees have clarity," says Koula Vasilopoulos, a district president at Robert Half (the parent company of OfficeTeam). "Managers should clearly articulate [explain] standards for what is appropriate; formally through corporate policies, and informally, leading by example through their own attire. With their guidance, employees will be able to make clothing choices that showcase their confidence and professionalism."

The best strategy for casual Friday: Be conservative at first, observe what your coworkers are wearing, and then adjust your wardrobe accordingly. That way, you'll fit in while still getting the chance to dress a little more casually.

Find out how dressing up at work can improve your job performance.

ON THE WEB: DRESSING FOR WORK

Business Casual Attire
https://career.vt.edu/job-search/presenting_yourself/attire/business-casual.html
Business Casual Outfits
www.askmen.com/fashion/trends/21_fashion_men.html

Dress Business Casual—Men
https://oureverydaylife.com/dress-business-casual-men-12108144.html
What Is Business Casual? Our Guide
www.monster.com/career-advice/article/business-casual-dress
A Relaxed, Casual Dress Code for Work
www.thebalance.com/a-relaxed-casual-dress-code-1919378
What Does Business Casual Attire Mean?
www.thebalance.com/what-is-business-casual-attire-2061168

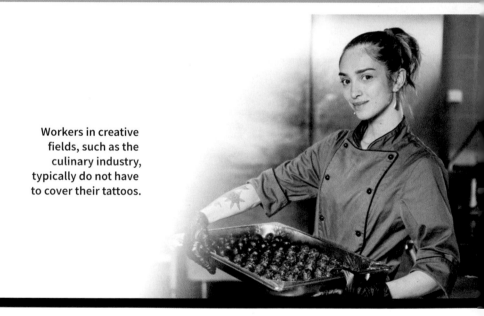

Workers in creative fields, such as the culinary industry, typically do not have to cover their tattoos.

TATTOOS AND BODY PIERCINGS

Thirty-eight percent of 18- to 29-year-olds have at least one tattoo, according to the Pew Research Center. Seventy-two percent of those tattoos were generally covered and not visible. Additionally, 23 percent of respondents had piercings in locations other than an earlobe. It's clear that tattoos and piercings are becoming more popular today. They serve as a form of self-expression and creativity, and some people even view tattoos as a form of art. But as a new worker, you should realize that not every employer will appreciate your attempts at individualism. Thirty-seven percent of hiring managers surveyed by specialty skincare boutique skinfo cited tattoos as the third most likely physical attribute that limits career potential. Like it or not, that's a fact in the workplace—especially in corporate settings and in some service- and sales-oriented industries. On the other hand, more creative employers may not care one bit about your tattoos and piercings.

DID YOU KNOW?

Forty-two percent of people of all ages feel that visible tattoos at work are inappropriate. This percentage was higher (63 percent) for people age 60 years and older, while it was much lower (22 percent) for those ages 18 – 25.

Thirty-six percent of people outside the United States feel that visible tattoos are inappropriate in the workplace.

Fourteen percent of people with tattoos regret getting a tattoo.

Source: skinfo

Before you head to a job interview and/or start a job, it's important to determine your target employer's policy regarding these body adornments. You can visit the employer's website to view photos of employees to determine the acceptance level for tattoos and piercings. You can also use social media sites to reach out to past or current employees of the company to get answers.

Here are a few general rules regarding tattoos and piercings, although remember that policies vary by employer:

- Many large companies prefer or mandate (require) that employees cover their tattoos.
- Always cover visible tattoos that feature profanity or offensive images.
- Women should not display more than one piercing in each ear. Some career experts advise men to not wear earrings, although this policy varies by employer.

- Multiple piercings—including those in the eyebrow, lip, ears, and nose—may be acceptable at creative employers.

Bottom line: Do your research to determine the policy at your target company. If the policy restricts tattoos and piercings, follow the rules, cover them (tattoos), or remove them (piercings). It's worth a bit of sacrifice to get your dream job.

THE MOST TATTOO-FRIENDLY U.S. COMPANIES

- Albertsons
- Amazon
- Anthropologie
- Applebee's
- Barnes & Noble
- Best Buy
- Big Lots
- Borders
- Burlington Coat Factory
- Claire's
- Dunkin' Donuts
- FedEx
- Forever 21
- Google
- Half Price Books
- Hard Rock Cafe/Hotel
- Home Depot
- Hot Topic/Torrid
- IKEA
- Journeys
- Kohl's
- Lowe's
- Lush Cosmetics
- MAC Cosmetics
- Petco
- Piercing Pagoda
- Sally Beauty Supply
- Spencer's Gifts
- Staples
- Ticketmaster
- Tokyo Joe's
- Trader Joe's
- UPS
- Whole Foods
- Zappos

Source: skinfo

TRUE OR FALSE ANSWERS: ARE YOU AN APPEARANCE EXPERT?

1. It's a good idea to periodically check your work clothing for excessive wear or other issues.
   True. Even your favorite "power suit" will wear out eventually, get a stain, or otherwise become worn or damaged and unwearable.

Styles also change each year, so it's a good idea to not only periodically review your clothes for excessive wear and stains but also to determine if the article of clothing is still in fashion.

2. Casual Friday rules are the same regardless of where you work.
False. Casual Friday rules vary greatly depending on your employer. For example, the casual Friday dress code at one employer might consist of khakis and polo shirts, while at another, employees may not be required to wear a tie and suit coat but still have to wear dress slacks and a sport coat.

3. Having a tattoo is fine in all workplaces.
False. Some companies have policies that require workers to cover visible tattoos. At others, workers are encouraged to express their individuality and display their tattoos and piercings.

RESEARCH PROJECT

Take a visual inventory of your closet. Identify items of clothing that are appropriate for the workplace, and put some outfit combinations together. Ask your parents for guidance. Pick ten items of clothing that would not be appropriate. List them on a piece of paper and detail, in a short sentence for each, why they are inappropriate (e.g., too revealing, too tight, collars frayed, etc.).

TEXT-DEPENDENT QUESTIONS

1. What did Amari do wrong regarding his workplace appearance?
2. Can you name three rules to follow regarding one's work wardrobe?
3. What is casual Friday? What can you wear on that day?

WORDS TO UNDERSTAND

acumen: skill or ability

image consultant: someone who gives advice to people regarding ways in which they can improve their confidence, body language, public speaking ability, and personal appearance, among other areas

jargon: special words used by members of a particular profession or group that are hard to understand by outsiders

politician: a person who has been elected to or is running for office (such as mayor, senator, or president)

CHAPTER 3

TEN TRAITS OF AN INVALUABLE EMPLOYEE

STAY-LATE SHEILA

Sheila, a young engineer at a large environmental engineering firm, was known for staying late at work to complete projects. This habit was so prevalent that her coworkers began good-naturedly calling her Stay-Late Sheila. Some of her teammates who were hired at the same time suggested that maybe she was overdoing it. Sheila laughed and replied, "Other people stay late sometimes too. I like working hard, and I can sleep well at night knowing that my extra effort has brought the team one step closer to completing the project." Sometimes extra effort goes unnoticed, but not in Sheila's case. Several times, her boss stopped by the office in the early evening after meeting clients for dinner and noticed Sheila hard at work. He was impressed, and during her next employee review, Sheila received high ratings, a promotion to project leader, and a raise. As for her teammates who named her Stay-Late Sheila, their reviews were fine, but they didn't receive a promotion or a pay raise. It's a cliché, but true: Good work pays off.

TRUE OR FALSE?
DO YOU HAVE THE SKILLS
TO SUCCEED ON THE JOB?

1. It doesn't matter if your work emails have grammatical errors as long as you get the point across.
2. Most companies want employees who can work on their own without any interaction with their boss or coworkers.
3. You can't be a leader if you're new to a job.

Test yourself as you read. See the end of this chapter for True or False Answers.

KEY SKILLS FOR JOB SUCCESS

A strong work ethic is just one of many soft skills you need to develop to stand out in the workplace. Yet despite the importance of soft skills, many executives believe that new employees lack these abilities. In fact, nearly four in ten corporate executives and almost half of leaders of academic institutions say new hires lack the soft skills they need to perform at a high level, according to a Bloomberg Next study sponsored by Workday. (Workday is an on-demand, cloud-based financial management and human capital management software vendor.) The fact that many new workers are deficient in these traits suggests that there will be great opportunities for those who actually do possess them. In addition to a strong work ethic, here are some other key qualities of employees who stand out in the workplace.

WRITTEN COMMUNICATION SKILLS

When you turned in your last college term paper, you may have thought that was the last time you'd need your writing skills. But think again. Employers ranked writing ability as the trait they seek most on résumés, according to a survey by the National Association of Colleges and Employers. And if employers want job applicants to demonstrate good writing skills on a résumé, it's a sure thing that this ability is also important for career success. On the job, you will frequently be asked to write reports, memos, and many other documents. You'll also need to be skilled at writing concise, clear emails. At some employers, you will be asked to write speeches, press releases, marketing copy, scripts for sales presentations, or social media posts. A small library worth of books has been published that will help you develop your writing skills, but here are a few quick tips to keep in mind to create well-crafted work documents.

- Write with a purpose. Most work documents require you to get to the point, not write a Stephen King novel. Your boss and coworkers are short on time just like you, so you should cover the topic in as few words as possible in order to convey what you want or think.
- Use the active voice when writing.
- Pay close attention to grammar and spelling. Errors in these areas send a message that you are careless and not detail-oriented. Some people may even question your intelligence if your reports and memos are full of grammatical errors.
- Never use slang or profanity.
- Avoid using industry-specific acronyms unless everyone on your team knows them.
- Don't use long words when a shorter one will work just as effectively… or well (e.g., utilize vs. use; ascertain vs. find out; convene vs. meet; commence vs. begin; etc.).
- Use transitions (e.g., however, because, etc.) to move between instructions or ideas so that the reader is not confused.

- Don't use emoticons; they are inappropriate in business writing.
- In reports and emails, use bullets when you have groups of three ideas or more.
- Proofread anything you've written before you send it to your boss or colleagues. Check it for content, clarity, and conciseness, as well as for proper punctuation and grammar.

READ MORE ABOUT IT: BUILDING YOUR WRITING SKILLS

Business Writing for Dummies by Natalie Canavor

Business Writing Scenarios by Jon Ramsey

Business Writing Today: A Practical Guide by Natalie Canavor

Writing That Works: Communicating Effectively on the Job by Walter E. Oliu, Charles T. Brusaw, and Gerald J. Alred

Writing Well for Business Success: A Complete Guide to Style, Grammar, and Usage at Work by Sandra E. Lamb

Two factory workers tackle a production problem.

PROBLEM-SOLVING SKILLS

Ken was rapidly developing a reputation as a problem solver at work. Although he had only been on the job for six months, he'd already created a plan that streamlined the development process for a new video game his team was creating, kept the project on schedule when two members of his team went down unexpectedly with chicken pox, and even found open-source software that the team could use to replace the expensive proprietary software they had been using. Some of his teammates nicknamed him "Can-Do Ken," which made him laugh. "It's no big deal," he said to them. "I just like solving problems and finding ways to get the job done better." But it was a big deal to Ken's boss, who took notice and made him the project lead on the next assignment.

As you can see, workers with good problem-solving skills get ahead in the workplace. You can be like Ken and become a master problem solver simply by thinking creatively about your team's work processes and tools and finding ways to make them better. Problem-solving doesn't always come easy. Someone else on your team may have already had your idea, or your proposed solution may not work. The key is to take the time to carefully assess each workplace challenge, ascertain what has already been tried to fix the problem, and then think creatively to come up with potential solutions.

The ability to solve problems may seem like a basic tool in anyone's skill set, but it's not. Sixty percent of employers surveyed by PayScale.com rated recent college graduates as lacking in critical thinking and problem-solving skills. Work hard to develop these abilities so that you're not part of that 60 percent. Doing so will pay off in more ways than you can imagine.

DID YOU KNOW?

Business executives and leaders at academic institutions ranked the ability to work as part of a team as the most important soft skill for workplace success, according to a Bloomberg Next study sponsored by Workday.

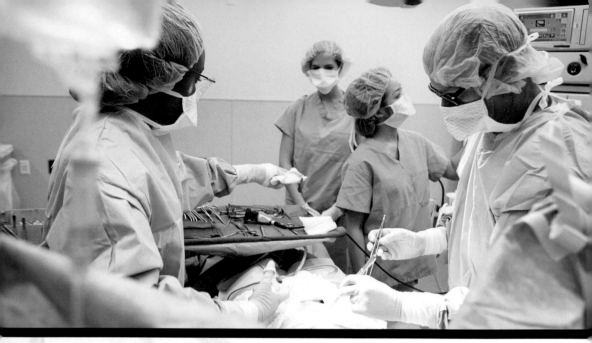

The ability to perform effectively as a member of a team is important
in all jobs, but especially so if you work as part of a surgical team.

ABILITY TO WORK IN A TEAM

Companies and other organizations are comprised of a variety of teams that
must work together to meet goals. If teams fail to gel, projects can be delayed,
sales goals may not be met, and the work environment may grow toxic. It's
in the best interest of every organization to create an atmosphere in which
employees get along and teams work well together. "Effective teamwork is good
for business," explained Michelle Burke, the CEO of the Energy Catalyst Group (a
teamwork consulting business), in the Huffington Post. "Stronger relationships
between team members, greater job satisfaction, energized employees and a
more engaged workforce are just a few of the benefits…When team members
meet their goals, everyone wins."

You will be a member of many teams during your career, and it's important
that you develop the ability to work well in these groups. You'll need a
combination of excellent communication (including listening) skills, patience,
negotiating ability, adaptability, and many other traits to be a good team member.

You'll also need to learn how to work well with people from diverse backgrounds, including those with disabilities, coworkers of different genders, and those from different religious, ethnic, and cultural groups. The following books will help you learn more about working successfully on a team. There are also many resources on the internet.

- *365 Low or No Cost Workplace Teambuilding Activities: Games and Exercises Designed to Build Trust & Encourage Teamwork Among Employees* by John N. Peragine
- *Collaborating with the Enemy: How to Work with People You Don't Agree with or Like or Trust* by Adam Kahane
- *Illustrated Course Guides: Teamwork & Team Building: Soft Skills for a Digital Workplace* by Jeff Butterfield
- *Powerhouse: 13 Teamwork Tactics that Build Excellence and Unrivaled Success* by Kristine Lilly, Dr. John Gillis Jr., et al.

INITIATIVE

Juan has always been the kind of person who takes initiative. "In high school," he recalls, "I worked as a stock clerk and cashier at a drug store. When my shift started, I got right to work. I emptied the garbage cans, swept the floors, refilled empty shelves with products, and did many other tasks without being asked. One day, my boss told me, 'Juan, I really like how you get right to work when you start your shift, unlike some of your coworkers who start their day with a cup of coffee and talk about whatever they did last night. I love that you take initiative and look for things to fix and improve rather than me having to tell you.'"

Juan maintained this "initiative mind-set" when he started working as an engineering technician at an automaker. He would conduct research to learn about new design software and industry practices that were saving other companies money, and he would suggest these improvements to his boss. If he had downtime, he would work on upcoming projects so that he would not be so hard-pressed to complete them by the deadline. Juan even took the initiative to find his own mentor at the company, who helped him learn the ropes and become a better employee.

As a new hire, you should work hard to be like Juan. Here are some ways to take initiative, become a valuable member of your team, and get noticed:

- Always do more than is required of you
- Speak up and share your ideas with your boss and colleagues
- Look for opportunities to take initiative in your department and throughout your company
- Learn new skills so that you will be ready to take initiative when the opportunity arises

ANALYTICAL/QUANTITATIVE SKILLS

People use analytical skills to gather and assess information, make decisions, develop strategies to improve an organization's products or services, complete projects effectively, and perform many other tasks. Analytical skills are used to assess both qualitative information, which is subjective and based on observation and interpretation, and quantitative information, which is numerical, measurable data. Everyone has some ability to think analytically and quantitatively, but some people are more proficient than others. If you're worried about your skills in these areas, try these basic suggestions to improve your abilities:

- Participate in active reading. Your goal while engaging in this activity is not reading for pleasure; instead, it's to ask questions about the content and how your views or beliefs match up with those of the author. How has the book made you feel? Has it made you question some belief or bedrock piece of knowledge that you took as gospel? If a book (or movie, play, or other creative work, for that matter) has changed the way you think, that's good, because your mind is expanding and growing to view things in a different way.

- Develop your mathematical skills by doing sudoku puzzles and games that require you to use logic and analysis.
- Keep a journal and comment on and analyze current events, books that you read, movies that you see, and interactions with friends or colleagues.
- Don't be afraid to mix some random, creative brainstorming sessions into these more logical approaches to solving problems. Some of the best solutions combine both creative and analytical thought processes.

Developing strong oral communication skills is especially important if your job duties include representing your company at industry conferences.

VERBAL COMMUNICATION SKILLS

If you break into a cold sweat at the thought of public speaking—whether it's to a small group or a room of 500 people—don't feel badly. Studies show that approximately 75 percent of people have a fear of speaking in public. Unless you work in a job that requires no interaction with colleagues, customers, or clients—very few of these jobs exist, by the way—you will need to develop strong oral communication skills. Try the following to improve this skill.

- Listen to and observe coworkers who have reputations as good verbal communicators, and try to imitate their presentation style. You might even consider asking them for advice. These people may have been afraid of speaking in public at one time.

- If asked to present your work at a meeting, write down some points that you want to cover and practice what you will say with friends or family members. Ask them to critique your presentation. Some people even record themselves so that they can review the recording several times to work on different areas of their presentation.

- When speaking, take a deep breath and speak slowly. Make good eye contact with everyone at the table (or representative audience members if you are presenting to a large crowd).

- Demonstrate positive body language: Sit or stand up straight to send a message of confidence.

- If you are asked to speak to a large audience, understand what they want to hear. For example, if you're a scientist and your company asks you to take a group of **politicians** on a tour of your laboratory, you should recognize that these people do not want to hear a bunch of complex scientific **jargon**. They want to know about the basic functions of the laboratory, what types of products your company develops, and how those products help make people's lives easier or better.

- If public speaking is still challenging, consider working with an **image consultant**. Some people even join Toastmasters International, a nonprofit educational organization that was founded in 1924 to help people improve their communication and leadership skills.

LEADERSHIP ABILITY

When we think of leaders, images of well-known politicians, CEOs, religious leaders, human rights activists, and army generals come to mind. But you don't need to be a newsmaker—or even in a position of power—to be a leader. If you're a new employee, you can demonstrate leadership and set an example for others by not being late for work, not copying the actions of your colleagues if they break company rules, staying late to complete projects, dealing with people in a polite, respectful, and ethical manner, and doing many other things. Young workers who demonstrate these traits are often the first to be considered for promotions and raises. Some organizations even have leadership development programs that identify rising stars. These programs provide training courses and pair participants with mentors.

DETAIL-ORIENTED PERSONALITY

Employers seek workers who meet deadlines, are experts in the most minute details of projects, remember people's names, can retrieve information from their paper or digital file folders at a moment's notice, don't repeat the same mistakes, and never turn in error-filled or factually incorrect memos and reports.

Fashion designers need both creative ability and a detail-oriented personality to be successful in their careers.

Being a detail-oriented person may seem hard, but it's really not. Here are a few suggestions to improve this highly sought-after trait:

- Use time-management and project-planning software to develop your schedule and organize your workload.
- As a new employee, keep a journal of the names of coworkers you meet, their departments, and their job titles. Add personal information (birthdays, names of spouses and children, hobbies, etc.) to the journal so that you have as much information as possible about each person. As you gather intel, pay special attention to your boss and members of your department.
- Keep your computer files and your workspace well organized so that you can find information quickly when asked.
- Proofread all office correspondence and reports several times to make sure that they are free of grammatical, spelling, and other errors.

ADAPTABILITY

Changing deadlines. Evolving job titles. New team members. Company mergers. These are just a few of the issues you might encounter on the job. How you respond to these and other challenges will go a long way toward how you are perceived by your boss and coworkers. The ability to adapt is so important that leaders at academic institutions and business executives ranked it as the fourth most important soft skill for workplace success, according to a Bloomberg Next study sponsored by Workday. Adaptability seems like something that is part of your personality or not, but you can actually work to improve your adaptability acumen. Here are a few tips.

- Don't treat every rule change, moved-up deadline, or other bump in the road as a disaster. Stay calm, avoid complaining about shifting work situations to your colleagues, and try to view change as an opportunity to grow and learn new skills.

- As changes are made, adopt an attitude of "present-mindedness," which means that you focus on excelling at the aspects of your job that you can control and try to pay as little attention as possible to things you can't (new work teams, company mergers, etc.).

- If you really don't agree with a planned change (such as switching to a different type of software to do your job), develop a list of fact-based reasons that can convince your boss that the old way is best. Present your argument in a calm, respectful manner, but embrace the new way of doing things if your boss still plans to make the switch.

In the end, those who oppose changes at work don't usually get promoted or prosper. They develop a reputation as negative people who are unwilling to try new things or be flexible when evolving customer demand or business trends make adjustments necessary.

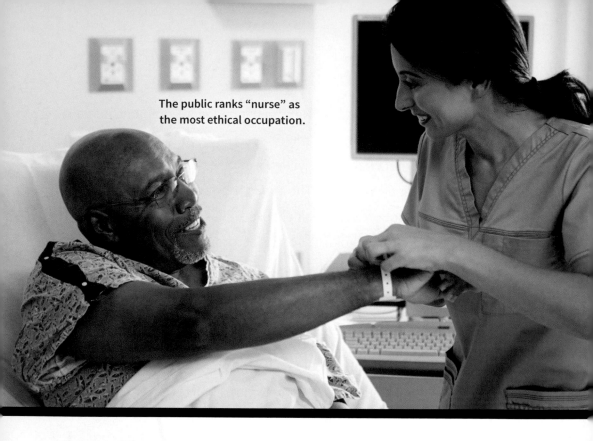

The public ranks "nurse" as the most ethical occupation.

THE MOST AND LEAST TRUSTED PROFESSIONS

The public views some professions as having higher honesty and ethical standards than others. Here are the most and least respected professions, according to a survey of Americans by the Gallup organization.

Most Trusted
1. Nurses: Cited by 82% of respondents
2. Military officers: 71%
3. Grade school teachers: 66%
4. Medical doctors: 65%
5. Pharmacists: 62%
6. Police officers: 56%

Least Trusted
1. Lobbyists: 8%
2. Business executives: 16%
3. Lawyers: 18%
4. Television reporters: 23%
5. Local officeholders: 24%
6. Bankers: 25%

STRONG ETHICS

Ethics are the unwritten rules that control how we treat one another and interact with the world. The word "ethics" comes from the Greek word *ethos*, meaning "character." What is right or wrong varies to some degree in each culture, but most people agree that it is wrong to lie, steal, and hurt or kill others.

Ethical misconduct in the workplace occurs more often than you probably think. A survey of workers at large companies (90,000+ employees) by the Ethics & Compliance Initiative, a group of organizations committed to creating and sustaining high-quality ethics and compliance programs, found that 23 percent of respondents were pressured by others to compromise their ethical standards and 62 percent observed misconduct. Here are a few examples of such situations:

- Your boss asks you to lie on productivity reports so that it looks like your department accomplished more than it did.
- You may be tempted to take office supplies for your own personal use, or if you work at a grocery store or restaurant, you may be tempted to help yourself to free food or drinks.
- Your boss may ask you to lie about product pricing or delivery schedules in order to land a new customer.
- Your coworker may ask you to "look the other way" if they leave work early or frequently take care of personal business on company time.
- You may be tempted to "borrow" the work of a colleague and claim it as your own.
- You notice that your coworker is sexually harassing a colleague, but he pressures you to not take the matter to your boss.
- Your manager asks you to do something illegal in exchange for a pay raise or promotion.

You will be involved in many situations in the workplace in which your personal ethics are tested. First of all, you should never violate the rules of your organization or break your personal ethical code (your view of right and wrong). You should also resist the temptation to help your coworkers or boss break company rules or the law. Doing so may result in the loss of your job or—if breaking an actual law—criminal prosecution.

TRUE OR FALSE ANSWERS: DO YOU HAVE THE SKILLS TO SUCCEED ON THE JOB?

1. It doesn't matter if your work emails have grammatical errors as long as you get the point across.
    False. "Spelling, grammar, and accuracy mistakes can be a huge distraction for a reader and can easily injure your credibility," advises *Fast Company* in an article about the importance of sending error-free emails.

2. Most companies want employees who can work on their own without any interaction with their boss or coworkers.
    True and False. Employers want independent workers who can accomplish tasks on their own without hovering bosses, but they also want employees who have excellent communication, interpersonal, listening, and collaboration skills so that they can work effectively as a member of a team.

3. You can't be a leader if you're new to a job.
    False. As a new hire straight out of school, you won't have the title of CEO or department manager, but you can still demonstrate leadership skills such as providing a good example to others, helping less experienced members of your team with difficult tasks, and leading the way with new ideas and approaches to solving problems. People who act like leaders often eventually become leaders at their companies.

Work hard to develop a good reputation in your office. Above, a young
worker is congratulated for being named "Employee of the Month."

RESEARCH PROJECT

What are your strongest and weakest soft skills? List three skills
that need work and write a 500-word essay that details how you
will improve them. Additionally, consider taking classes, reading
books, and participating in other activities that help you hone
these traits.

TEXT-DEPENDENT QUESTIONS

1. Can you name four ways to improve your writing skills?
2. What did you learn in this chapter about the address
   Lincoln gave at Gettysburg?
3. What are some examples of how you will need to be adapt-
   able on the job?

finite: having limits or boundaries

performance review: a regular review of an employee's job performance

rapport: a close relationship between two people that involves empathy and mutual understanding

sales lead: a person or business that may be a candidate to purchase goods or services from another business

succinct: said or written in a short, concise way

CHAPTER 4

HOW TO GET ALONG WELL WITH YOUR BOSS

THE IMPORTANCE OF GETTING ALONG WITH YOUR BOSS

During your career, you will probably have many bosses. Some will be easy to work for; others will be terrible taskmasters. Some will be happy and upbeat, while others will be worrywarts and prone to bad moods when things don't go well. You might even have a manager who is all of these things and more during a particular day or week!

Your boss plays a major role in your work life. You will spend a lot of time with them each day, and the strength of your relationship directly influences how quickly you will advance at your employer. Thus, developing a good relationship with your supervisor is critical for career success.

HOW TO DEVELOP A GOOD RELATIONSHIP WITH YOUR MANAGER

There's no getting around it: You need to get along well with your boss to get ahead. That doesn't mean that you have to be best friends, but you need to develop a good working relationship. "Nobody, but nobody is more important to your job satisfaction and happiness, your progress and development on the job than your boss," says Roger Fritz, the author of *Power of a Positive Attitude: Discovering the Key to Success*. So how do you get in good with your supervisor? There are many ways to develop a strong relationship with your manager, but here are some of the best strategies.

Know your boss's likes and dislikes. Is your manager a morning or afternoon person? Do they like to hear good news or bad news first? What's their preferred form of communication (email, telephone, in person)? You get the idea. The more that you learn about your boss's personality and work preferences, the more you can mold your behavior to match these traits.

Never make your boss look bad during meetings, even if you strongly disagree with what they are saying.

Never make your boss look bad. Don't talk negatively about your supervisor behind their back. Don't go over your boss's head with complaints—unless they are serious ones that involve ethical violations or their inappropriate behavior toward you. Share work-related bad news with your boss immediately when you receive it so they do not feel blindsided by new developments.

Be loyal to your boss. In a subtle way, let your manager know that you are on their side. If you hear someone bad-mouthing your supervisor or conveying incorrect information about your department, tell your boss what you heard.

Make your manager's life easier. Try to understand your supervisor's goals, and work to support them. Think about ways that you can help your boss do their job better. For example, you might take the initiative and do some research on a new manufacturing process you both discussed. Remember that your boss has a boss. Perhaps you can casually spread the word about your manager's achievements or competency in a way that reaches the higher-ups.

Don't question your manager's authority. Never be disrespectful or dismissive when your boss presents an idea or gives you an assignment—especially if you are in a meeting. If you believe a different approach is warranted, explain so calmly and respectfully and present a fact-based argument that supports your opinion. Never hold a grudge against your supervisor if you strongly disagree about something. Move on, act professionally, and try to find common ground on the next project that you tackle.

THE SKILLS THAT NEW GRADUATES MOST OFTEN LACK

Eighty-seven percent of recent grads said they were "well prepared" for the workforce, while only 50 percent of managers felt that way, according to a PayScale.com survey of 63,924 managers and 14,167 recent graduates. Here were the percentages of managers who felt new hires were deficient in a particular soft or hard skill:

- Critical thinking/problem-solving: 60%
- Attention to detail: 56%
- Communication: 46%
- Leadership: 44%
- Writing proficiency: 44%
- Ownership of mistakes: 44%
- Public speaking: 39%
- Interpersonal skills/teamwork: 36%
- Data analysis (Excel, Tableau, Python, etc.): 36%
- Industry-specific software (Salesforce, computer-aided design, QuickBooks, etc.): 34%
- Grit: 25%
- Mathematics: 19%
- Curiosity: 16%

When you have problems with your boss, it's easy to think they are the issue. But this survey suggests that some new hires need to take an honest look at their own skill set to make sure they are not the problem. This is something to keep in mind as you develop a relationship with your supervisor and try to stand out in the workplace.

Stay in frequent communication. It's tempting to steer clear of your boss, but that's the wrong approach. At the beginning of each day, you should check in with your supervisor about their goals for the day. And keep them updated about your progress on projects and accomplishments. "At the end of every week, I sent my manager a one-page memo that summarized what I had accomplished on various projects, what potential roadblocks I expected in the next week, and a completion time estimate for each project," explains Malcolm, an editor who worked at a large publishing company in New York City. "When I was promoted to managing editor, my manager cited my strong communication skills and detail-oriented personality as two important factors that fueled my promotion."

Tell the truth. Resist the urge to stretch the facts when it comes to your ability to meet deadlines or generate **sales leads**, or your skill at performing a particular task. If you've never used a specific type of machinery or software, say so. That way, you can get the training you need. Take responsibility for your mistakes. Bosses do not like surprises—especially those that negatively affect work schedules and your team's performance.

Learn how to talk to your boss about sensitive issues such as asking for a raise.

Recognize that your manager's time is finite. Your supervisor has many duties. They must meet with your colleagues, members of other departments, and the company's chief executives. They also have to complete their own work. When you meet with your boss, make sure that you are highly organized, have all the documents you need, and get right to the point. Keep emails and memos succinct so that your manager does not have to wade through unnecessary text to get the facts.

Arrive early and stay late. Bosses like to arrive at the office and see their employees already hard at work and ready to tackle the challenges of the day. Also, it never hurts to remain working after your shift ends. Your boss will be impressed by your work ethic, and the extra time you spend at the office will let you get a head start on the next day's tasks. Of course, if you're staying several hours after closing time every day, that suggests you are being assigned too much work or not managing your time well. In this instance, talk with your boss to try to resolve the situation.

Develop a good reputation in the office. By working hard, lending a hand without being asked, treating your coworkers with respect, dressing professionally, not complaining about your company or boss to coworkers, always meeting deadlines, and doing other positive things, your actions will reflect positively on your manager. If your supervisor hears good things about you, they will be more appreciative of your work and more likely to promote you or give you a raise.

Accept constructive criticism. There is always room for improvement in life. If your boss provides you with instruction on how you can do your job better, accept the constructive criticism graciously, thank them for their feedback, and vow to improve your job performance. Losing your temper or being dismissive in such a situation is the surest way to get on the wrong side of your manager.

WHAT TO DO IF YOU CAN'T GET ALONG WITH YOUR BOSS

Not every boss-employee relationship is a good one. You may have started out well, but the relationship slowly cooled due to issues on both sides. Maybe you've tried all of the things we discussed earlier in this chapter with no change. In this situation, you have two options: leave the organization to seek out a better fit, or try to fix the problem.

Keep in mind that many workers who are considered invaluable to their company or organization may have once had a poor relationship with their boss; however, they made the effort to fix the problem and rebuild the connection. You may be able to do the same, and here are some suggestions that can help:

- **Diagnose the problem.** Ask yourself the following questions: Am I doing something that annoys my boss? Have I disregarded their feedback or instructions on a particular project? Have I failed to address the performance issues my supervisor identified in my last **performance review?** Have I bad-mouthed my manager and has it somehow gotten back to them? If you answered "yes" to one or more of these questions, you must work to change your behavior and repair the relationship. If you're truly blameless, your boss may be having personal issues, may be facing pressures to meet productivity goals from top management, or may be experiencing other work or personal challenges. In this situation, it's best to continue working hard and be as empathetic and supportive as possible. Managers go through rough periods too. In time, the situation may resolve itself, and you may once again be on good terms with your boss.
- **Accept responsibility and apologize.** Meet with your boss to address any instances in which you did not perform well, ignored their advice, or otherwise acted in a way that negatively affected your working

relationship. Apologize for your actions and promise that you will do better. If your supervisor is willing to give you a second chance, work hard to be excellent in every way and be patient—it may take a while to win back your manager's trust.

- **Clarify your manager's expectations for you.** Ask your boss to reiterate how you can be a better employee, and work hard to meet their expectations.

- **Try to connect on a personal level.** Attempt to build a good **rapport** with your manager by discussing topics—such as sports, movies, vacation destinations, hobbies, and family—that are unrelated to work. You might even ask your supervisor out for coffee to try to get to know them on a personal level. But don't force this type of connection. Your instincts will tell you if there is the possibility of developing a personal relationship with your boss.

It's in your best interest to try to repair a damaged relationship with your boss. If you leave your employer, you will lose your seniority and have to begin building relationships and your reputation as a quality worker from scratch. For some, the grass is actually greener at a new employer. But for others, a far worse boss may be waiting in that corner office.

TRUE OR FALSE ANSWERS: DO YOU KNOW HOW TO BUILD A GOOD RELATIONSHIP WITH YOUR BOSS?

1. A healthy relationship between a manager and employee involves steady and open communication.
   True. A happy boss is one who is kept in the loop regarding the status of projects, potential roadblocks, and other issues.

2. It's important to be able to accept constructive criticism.
True. Most constructive criticism makes you a better employee in the long run.

3. If I'm having a problem with my boss, it may be my fault.
True and False. You may be the cause of the problem, or you may not. The situation could just boil down to having a bad boss. A survey by Monster.com found that 76 percent of workers who were openly seeking a new job were doing so because of a "toxic boss."

RESEARCH PROJECT

In your experience as a worker in summer jobs, internships, or other opportunities, what type of relationship did you have with your managers? Good? Bad? Just ok? Write a 250-word report about three major work or internship experiences that describes your relationship with your boss and their management style. If the relationship was just ok or bad, what would you do to fix it if you could go back in time? Take these lessons with you when you start your next job.

TEXT-DEPENDENT QUESTIONS

1. What are three ways to develop a good relationship with your boss?
2. Can you name five traits in which managers believe new hires are deficient?
3. If you have a problem with your supervisor, how do you diagnose the issue?

WORDS TO UNDERSTAND

clique: a small group of people who join together as a result of shared interests and then exclude others

Herculean: requiring great effort or strength

private sector: the part of the economy in which for-profit businesses operate without the direct oversight of the government

sartorial: relating to clothing and one's style of dress

CHAPTER 5

NAVIGATING OFFICE POLITICS AND OTHER CHALLENGES

MASTERING WORKPLACE CHALLENGES

You've successfully met the challenges of being a new employee. You're a **sartorial** superstar, a great communicator, a detail-oriented producer, and a good time manager, and you have other key soft and hard skills. You even get along with your boss. If you were an athlete, you'd be an all-star! But even if you're an all-star, there are things that are out of your control that may affect your performance. Members of your team may not get along with you; a colleague might harass you because of your race, religion, or other reasons;

your workplace might be unsafe; or you may face other obstacles. How you react to these challenges will directly influence your success on the job. In the following sections, you will learn about some of the biggest workplace issues and how to handle them.

TRUE OR FALSE?
ARE YOU PREPARED TO HANDLE
WORKPLACE CHALLENGES?

1. It's important to be on the right side when power struggles begin at your office.
2. Only women can be sexually harassed.
3. If you identify a safety issue at your work, the first steps you should take are to document it and bring it to the attention of your boss or the HR department.

Test yourself as you read. See the end of this chapter for True or False Answers.

Avoid participating in gossip in the workplace because it can destroy company morale.

OFFICE POLITICS

In a perfect world, you will get along great with your coworkers. But the world is not perfect, and workplaces are often disturbed by cliques, power struggles, gossip, and other issues that affect the job performance of employees and, even their overall mental and physical health. Some business leaders believe that a competitive, high-pressure work environment creates good results for a company, but this is untrue. According to the *Harvard Business Review*, "A large and growing body of research on positive organizational psychology demonstrates that not only is a cut-throat environment harmful to productivity over time, but that a positive environment will lead to dramatic benefits for employers, employees, and the bottom line."

How do you contribute to creating a positive environment? If your workplace is negative and stressful, it may seem like a Herculean task to turn the tide, but if you set a good example, others may follow. Here are some suggestions on how to do so:

- Never engage in negative conversations about your colleagues or your organization. If you have legitimate concerns about a coworker or a company policy, take them to your manager or the HR department.
- Don't take sides when power struggles occur between two people in your office. If asked, try to find positive things to say about each person.
- Don't join cliques or seek to exclude certain people in your office. Try to develop friendships with people of every race, culture, gender, religion, and employment level (from secretarial staff to top executives).
- Avoid discussing divisive issues such as politics, religion, and gun rights/control in the workplace. Save these discussions for friends and family.
- Avoid taking breaks or having lunch with people who are known to be negative influences in the workplace.

The following resources will help you learn more about and survive office politics:

Seven Ways to Use Office Politics Positively

www.mindtools.com/pages/article/newCDV_85.htm

Workplace Gossip: What Crosses the Line?

www.shrm.org/resourcesandtools/hr-topics/employee-relations/pages/office-gossip-policies.aspx

Office Politics: Get Ahead Without Playing Dirty

www.thebalance.com/office-politics-526247

Sexual harassment remains a serious issue in workplaces throughout the world.

SEXUAL AND OTHER TYPES OF HARASSMENT

Sexual harassment is a major problem in the workplace. Nineteen percent of American adults (both women and men) say they have been victims of sexual harassment while on the job, according to a CNBC All-America Survey. The U.S. Equal Employment Opportunity Commission (EEOC) says that sexual harassment can include "unwelcome sexual advances, requests for sexual favors, and other verbal or physical harassment of a sexual nature. Harassment does not have to be of a sexual nature, however, and can include offensive remarks about a person's sex."

There are also other types of workplace harassment, including physical threats or assaults, intimidation and any other acts that create a hostile or abusive workplace, insults, offensive photos and videos, offensive jokes, slurs, and name-calling. Many of these actions are fueled by dislike of a person's gender, sexual identity, religion, ethnicity, or culture.

Harassment can result in great mental and physical stress. It can also cause workers to underperform on the job and even leave their organizations. On a large scale, this type of environment can destroy the cohesiveness of work teams and create a toxic atmosphere.

Most companies have rules that prohibit employees from verbally attacking one another.

If you are harassed in any way, don't stand for it. Organizational policies and laws in some countries make this behavior illegal. Additionally, the #MeToo movement has helped shed light on the high levels of sexual harassment in the workplace and prompted many organizations and companies to create better policies to punish instigators and ensure harassment-free workplaces. But what do you do if you are harassed? Follow these steps to address the issue:

1. Confront the individual or people involved and tell them you consider their comments or actions to be harassment. Be sure to document what occurred, when and where it occurred, how you responded, the names of any witnesses, and what you said to the instigator and their response.

2. If this does not stop the behavior, follow your organization's harassment reporting protocol to address the issue. Be prepared to work with your organization's HR department regarding the situation.

3. If your company's internal procedures do not fix the issue, consider filing an administrative charge with the EEOC (if you live in the United States) or another civil rights enforcement or human rights agency. If the agency determines that you have been harassed but cannot resolve the issue with your employer, it will issue you a "right to sue" letter, which means that you can take your case to court.

Learn how to deal with difficult colleagues.

READ MORE ABOUT IT: FIGHTING DISCRIMINATION OR HARASSMENT IN THE WORKPLACE

The topic of harassment is much too complicated to address in a short chapter. The following books provide a deeper look at the issue:

Be Fierce: Stop Harassment and Take Your Power Back by Gretchen Carlson

The Essential Guide to Handling Workplace Harassment & Discrimination by Deborah C. England

Feminist Fight Club: A Survival Manual for a Sexist Workplace by Jessica Bennett

Sexual Harassment Online: Shaming and Silencing Women in the Digital Age by Tania G. Levey.

Exposed electrical wiring is just one type of unsafe work condition.

UNSAFE WORK CONDITIONS

You probably take it for granted that where you work or intern will be clean, well lit, climate-controlled, and otherwise comfortable and safe. But in some workplaces, employees are exposed to dangerous conditions. Some of these can cause workers to be injured or even die. In 2019, approximately 2.8 million nonfatal workplace injuries and illnesses occurred at **private sector** employers in the United States, according to the U.S. Bureau of Labor Statistics. Nearly 5,333 workers died on the job.

While some professions (e.g., police officer, firefighter, pilot) are by their nature more dangerous than others, all employers must provide reasonably safe working conditions for their employees. If you have concerns about workplace safety, do the following:

1. Document the issue, if possible, by taking photographs or video of the problem, or by summarizing the issue in a brief memo.

2. Bring your concerns to your supervisor or HR department.

3. If no action is taken, keep moving up your company's organizational structure until you get results, or consider consulting with an employment lawyer.

4. If this doesn't work, consider filing a complaint with the Occupational Safety and Health Administration (OSHA) (if you work in the United States) and request that the agency conduct an inspection of your workplace. Note: Be sure to file a complaint quickly because OSHA citations may only be issued for violations that currently exist or existed in the past six months. Visit www.osha.gov/workers/file-complaint to learn more about the process. If you live in another country, check with local, state, or national safety agencies for advice on filing a claim.

TRUE OR FALSE ANSWERS: ARE YOU PREPARED TO HANDLE WORKPLACE CHALLENGES?

1. It's important to be on the right side when power struggles begin at your office.

False. You should never take a side in this type of situation because you should stay out of other people's business and seek to remain a positive force in the office.

2. Only women can be sexually harassed.
   False. Ten percent of men reported in 2017 that they had been victims of sexual harassment in the workplace, according to the CNBC All-America Survey.

3. If you identify a safety issue at your work, the first steps you should take are to document it and bring it to the attention of your boss or the HR department.
   True. Don't try to remedy the issue yourself unless it's something simple, such as cleaning up a coffee spill.

RESEARCH PROJECT

Learn more about the various forms of sexual harassment in the workplace. Find some examples of what well-known companies and organizations are doing to prevent this issue. Write a 500-word report that summarizes your findings and present it to your class.

TEXT-DEPENDENT QUESTIONS

1. What are some topics that you should not discuss in the office?
2. What are the three steps to addressing sexual harassment in the workplace?
3. How many people are injured or become ill on the job in the United States each year?

accreditation: The process of being evaluated and approved by a governing body as providing excellent coursework, products, or services. Quality college and university educational programs are accredited.

application materials: Items such as a cover letter, resume, and letters of recommendation that one provides to employers when applying for a job or an internship.

apprenticeship: A formal training program that combines classroom instruction and supervised practical experience. Apprentices are paid a salary that increases as they obtain experience.

associate's degree: A degree that requires a two-year course of study after high school.

bachelor's degree: A degree that requires a four-year course of study after high school.

certificate: A credential that shows a person has completed specialized education, passed a test, and met other requirements to qualify for work in a career or industry. College certificate programs typically last six months to a year.

certification: A credential that one earns by passing a test and meeting other requirements. Certified workers have a better chance of landing a job than those who are not certified. They also often earn higher salaries than those who are not certified.

community college: A private or public two-year college that awards certificates and associates degrees.

consultant: An experienced professional who is self-employed and provides expertise about a particular subject.

cover letter: A one-page letter in which a job seeker summarizes their educational and professional background, skills, and achievements, as well as states their interest in a job.

doctoral degree: A degree that is awarded to an individual who completes two or three additional years of education after earning a master's degree. It is also known as a **doctorate**.

for-profit business: One that seeks to earn money for its owners.

fringe benefits: A payment or non-financial benefit that is given to a worker in addition to salary. These consist of cash bonuses for good work, paid vacations and sick days, and health and life insurance.

information interview: The process of interviewing a person about their career, whether in person, by phone, online, or by email.

internship: A paid or unpaid learning opportunity in which a student works at a business to obtain experience for anywhere from a few weeks to a year.

job interview: A phone, internet, or in-person meeting in which a job applicant presents their credentials to a hiring manager.

job shadowing: The process of following a worker around while they do their job, with the goal of learning more about a particular career and building one's network.

licensing: Official permission that is granted by a government agency to a person in a particular field (nursing, engineering, etc.) to practice in their profession. Licensing requirements typically involve meeting educational and experience requirements, and sometimes passing a test.

master's degree: A two-year, graduate-level degree that is earned after a student first completes a four-year bachelor's degree.

mentor: An experienced professional who provides advice to a student or inexperienced worker (mentee) regarding personal and career development.

minimum wage: The minimum amount that a worker can be paid by law.

nonprofit organization: A group that uses any profits it generates to advance its stated goals (protecting the environment, helping the homeless, etc.). It is not a corporation or other for-profit business.

professional association: An organization that is founded by a group of people who have the same career (engineers, professional hackers, scientists, etc.) or who work in the same industry (information technology, health care, etc.).

professional network: Friends, family, coworkers, former teachers, and others who can help you find a job.

recruiting firm: A company that matches job seekers with job openings.

registered apprenticeship: A program that meets standards of fairness, safety, and training established by the U.S. government or local governments.

résumé: A formal summary of one's educational and work experience that is submitted to a potential employer.

salary: Money one receives for doing work.

scholarship: Money that is awarded to students to pay for college and other types of education; it does not have to be paid back.

self-employed: Working for oneself as a small business owner, rather than for a corporation or other employer. Self-employed people must generate their own income and provide their own fringe benefits (such as health insurance).

soft skills: Personal abilities that people need to develop to be successful on the job—communication, work ethic, teamwork, decision-making, positivity, time management, flexibility, problem-solving, critical thinking, conflict resolution, and other skills and traits.

technical college: A public or private college that offers two- or four-year programs in practical subjects, such as the trades, information technology, applied sciences, agriculture, and engineering.

union: An organization that seeks to gain better wages, benefits, and working conditions for its members. Also called a **labor union** or **trade union**.

work-life balance: A healthy balance of time spent on the job and time spent with family and on leisure activities.

FURTHER READING

Dalio, Ray. *Principles: Life and Work*. New York: Simon & Schuster, 2017.

Gilad, Benjamin, and Mark Chussil. *The NEW Employee Manual: A No-Holds-Barred Look at Corporate Life*. Irvine, CA: Entrepreneur Press, 2019.

Kahane, Adam. *Collaborating with the Enemy: How to Work with People You Don't Agree with or Like or Trust*. Oakland, CA: Berrett-Koehler Publishers, 2017.

Trillo, Alejandro. *Vices and Virtues: Knowing, Accepting and Improving Yourself*. Liguori, MO: Liguori Publications, 2015.

INTERNET RESOURCES

www.sutterhealth.org/pamf/health/preteens/relationships-social-skills/etiquette
This resource provides etiquette advice for a variety of situations—from talking on the telephone to greeting people to table etiquette.

www.cnbc.com/id/100983070
Visit this website for seven body language tips in areas such as posture, handshakes, and standing position.

www.livecareer.com/quintessential/15-excelling-work-tips
This website provides fourteen tips on how to impress your boss.

https://www.thebalancecareers.com/a-formal-professional-dress-code-1919381
Visit this website to learn how to dress for work and interviews.

EDUCATIONAL VIDEO LINKS

Chapter 1
Learn what to do during your first ninety days on the job: http://x-qr.net/1J6X

Chapter 2
Find out how dressing up at work can improve your job performance: http://x-qr.net/1LgR

Chapter 4
Learn how to talk to your boss about sensitive issues such as asking for a raise: http://x-qr.net/1JXR

Chapter 5
Learn how to deal with difficult colleagues: http://x-qr.net/1LRQ

INDEX

A

adaptability, 47
analytical skills, 42–43

B

blue jeans, 26
body language, 12, 15, 44
body piercings, 30–32
bosses
    building relationships with, 53–55, 57–58
    communicating with, 16–19, 47, 57–58
    and ethics, 49–50
    first meeting, 13
    repairing relationships with, 59–60
Burke, Michelle, 40

C

casual. *See* dress codes
cell phones, 16
chief executive officers (CEOs), 7
clothing. *See* dress codes
communication
    body language, 12, 15, 44
    with bosses, 16–19, 47, 57–58
    verbal skills, 43–45
    written skills, 37–38, 46
commuting, 18
computers, use of, 16
continuing education classes, 20
coworkers
    and ethics, 49–50
    first meeting, 13, 15
    relationships with, 17–19, 46, 58
    teamwork, 39–41

D

denim, 26
detail-oriented, 45–46

dress codes

casual Fridays, 28–29
and cognitive abilities, 25
definitions of, 29–30
do's and don'ts, 25–27
first day, 12–13
importance of, 12–13, 24–25, 29
tattoos/body piercings, 30–32

E

elevator pitches, 15
ethics, 36, 48–50
Ethics & Compliance Initiative, 49
expectations
    of employers, 8
    of new employees, 7–8

F

first impressions, 11–12, 23–24
Fritz, Roger, 54

G

Gettysburg Address, 45
glossaries, 10, 22, 34, 52, 62, 72–74
Griffith, Tricia, 7
grooming, personal, 27–28

H

harassment, 66–69
hard skills and new hires, 56
hiring managers, 17, 31
hostile work environment, 67–69
human resources departments (HR), 13, 16

I

initiative, 41–42

L

leadership, 45
Lincoln, Abraham, 45

M

#MeToo, 67
mentors, 20

N

new job
    first day, 11–13, 15–16
    first month, 19–20
    first ninety days, 19
    first week, 17–18
    Janice's experience, 11–12

O

Occupational Safety and Health Administration (OSHA), 70
office layouts, 15, 19
office politics, 64–66
oral communication skills, 43–45
OSHA, 70

P

personal grooming, 27–28
positive attitudes, 15–16
problem-solving skills, 38–39
professions and respectability, 48

Q

qualitative/quantitative skills, 42–43

R

reports, 37–38
resources
    on harassment, 69
    on office politics, 66
    on teamwork, 41, 75
    on work attire, 29–30, 75

on workplace behaviors, 75
on writing skills, 38
résumés, 17
Rondeau, Chris, 7

S

safety in workplace, 69–70
sexual harassment, 66–69
soft skills
    adaptability, 47
    analytical/quantitative skills, 42–43
    detail-oriented, 45–46
    hiring managers seek, 17
    initiative, 41–42
    lack of in new hires, 36, 39, 56
    leadership, 45
    problem-solving skills, 38–39
    Stay-Late Sheila's experience, 35–36
    teamwork, 39–41
    verbal communication skills, 43–45
    work ethic, 36, 48–50
    written communication skills, 37–38, 46

T

tattoos, 30–32
teamwork, 39–41
Toastmasters International, 44

U

unsafe working conditions, 69–70

V

Vasilopoulos, Koula, 29
verbal communication skills, 43–45

W

wardrobes. *See* dress codes
work day
    length of, by country, 14

starting early, 13, 58

staying late, 15, 58

Stay-Late Sheila, 35–36

Workday (business), 36

work documents, 37–38

work ethic, 36, 48–50

workplace behaviors

overview, 6–9

resources on, 75

See also bosses; coworkers; dress codes; new job; soft skills

workplace challenges

harassment, 66–69

office politics, 64–66

unsafe working conditions, 69–70

written communication skills, 37–38, 46

AUTHOR BIOGRAPHY

Andrew Morkes has been a writer and editor for more than twenty-five years. He is the author of more than forty books and newsletters about college planning and careers, including many titles in the Careers in the Building Trades series, the *Vault Career Guide to Pharmaceuticals and Biotechnology,* the *College Spotlight newsletter, and They Teach That in College!?: A Resource Guide to More Than 100 Interesting College Majors,* which was selected as one of the best books of the year by the library journal *Voice of Youth Advocates*. He is also the author and publisher of "The Morkes Report: College and Career Planning Trends" blog.

PHOTO CREDITS